First World War
and Army of Occupation
War Diary
France, Belgium and Germany

34 DIVISION
Divisional Troops
Royal Army Medical Corps
Divisional Field Ambulance Workshop Unit
8 January 1916 - 31 March 1916

WO95/2454/1

The Naval & Military Press Ltd
www.nmarchive.com
Published in association with The National Archives

Published by

The Naval & Military Press Ltd

Unit 10 Ridgewood Industrial Park,

Uckfield, East Sussex,

TN22 5QE England

Tel: +44 (0) 1825 749494

www.naval-military-press.com

www.nmarchive.com

This diary has been reprinted in facsimile from the original. Any imperfections are inevitably reproduced and the quality may fall short of modern type and cartographic standards.

© **Crown Copyright**
Images reproduced by permission of The National Archives, London, England, 2015.

Contents

Document type	Place/Title	Date From	Date To
Heading	WO95/2454/1		
Heading	34th Division 34t Fd Amb W'Shop Unit Jan-Mar 1916		
Heading	34th F.A.W.U. Jan Feb Mar 1916		
Heading	34th F.A.W.U. Vols. 1.2		
Miscellaneous	War Diary 34th Divisional Field Ambulance Workshop Unit. From 8th January 1916 To 31st January 1916 (Volume 1)		
War Diary	Avonmouth	08/01/1916	08/01/1916
War Diary	Southampton	09/01/1916	09/01/1916
War Diary	Rouen	10/01/1916	12/01/1916
War Diary	Blangy	13/01/1916	13/01/1916
War Diary	Arcques	14/01/1916	14/01/1916
War Diary	Renescure	20/01/1916	26/01/1916
War Diary	Morbecque	26/01/1916	26/01/1916
Miscellaneous	War Diary 34th Divisional Field Ambulance Workshop Unit From 1st February To 29th February 1916 Volume 1		
War Diary	Estaires	21/02/1916	24/02/1916
Miscellaneous	34th Divisional Field Ambulance Workshop Unit From 1st March 1916 (Volume. 1)		
War Diary	Steenwerck	01/03/1916	31/03/1916

WO 95/2454 (1)

WO 95/2454 (2)

34TH DIVISION

34T FD AMB W'SHOP UNIT

JAN – MAR 1916

34th YAWU

3rd YAWU

Jan
Feb } 1916
Mar

by F.R.a.W.U.
vols: 1, 2

WAR DIARY
or
INTELLIGENCE SUMMARY.

(Erase heading not required.)

Army Form C. 2118.

Place	Date	Hour	Summary of Events and Information	Remarks and references to Appendices
			Confidential

War Diary

of

34th Divisional Field Ambulance Workshop Unit

from 8th January 1916 to 31st January 1916

(Volume 1) | |

WAR DIARY
or
INTELLIGENCE SUMMARY.

(Erase heading not required.)

Army Form C. 2118.

34th Div F.A.W.U.

Place	Date	Hour	Summary of Events and Information	Remarks and references to Appendices
AVONMOUTH	8-1-16		Officer Commanding & 66 N.C.Os & men left AVONMOUTH by train for SOUTHAMPTON and camped at Rest Camp, SOUTHAMPTON for the night of 8th/9th January. Also, 5 N.C.Os & men, 21 Ambulances. W.D. NUMBERS:- A.18324; A.18317; A.18325; A.18326; A.18323; A.18321; A.18318; A.18320; A.18313; A.18319; A.18315; A.18314; A.6322; A.18312; A.18316; A.18331; A.18328; A.18330; A.18327; A.18329; A.18329; 3 Lorries i.e., 1 Workshop. W.D. No. 21471, 1 Store W.D. No. 21470; 1 Supply - 30cwt - W.D. No. 21472; 1 Car Vauxhall W.D. No. M.18333; 3 Motor Cycles. Nos. C.22568; C.22589; C.22590. embarked at AVONMOUTH on S.S. BLACKWELL at 7-45 A.M.	

Capt. A.S.C.
O.C. 34th Divl Supply Column

WAR DIARY or INTELLIGENCE SUMMARY.

Army Form C. 2118.

34th Divl. F.A.W.U

Place	Date	Hour	Summary of Events and Information	Remarks and references to Appendices
SOUTHAMPTON	9-1-16		Officer Commanding and 66 N.C.Os & men embarked at SOUTHAMPTON on S.S. CAESEREA at 3:30 pm	

J. P. Brockbank Capt. A.S.C.
O.C. 34T Divl. Supply Column

WAR DIARY or INTELLIGENCE SUMMARY.

Army Form C. 2118.

2nd Div. S.A.W.U.

Place	Date	Hour	Summary of Events and Information	Remarks and references to Appendices
ROUEN	10-1-16		Officer Commanding & 66 N.C.O's & men disembarked at ROUEN and marched to M.O. for Inspection. No cases of Venereal reported & men passed fit, afterwards proceeding to M.T. Rest Camp. Company deficiencies - 1 Interpreter.	

Capt. A.S.C.
O/C 2nd Divl. Supply Column

WAR DIARY
or
INTELLIGENCE SUMMARY.
(Erase heading not required.)

Army Form C. 2118.

34th Div¹ F.T.W.U.

Place	Date	Hour	Summary of Events and Information	Remarks and references to Appendices
ROUEN.	11-1-16		Officer 5 N.C.O's & men, 7 Ambulances, 3 lorries, 1 car, & 3 motor cycles disembarked at ROUEN at 11 a.m. and reported to Embarkation Officer. N.C.O's & men proceeded to M.O. for Inspection - all passed fit. ~~Company~~ Unit, paid.	

J.P. Birk̄ Capt. A.S.C.
O.C 34th Div¹ Supply Column.

WAR DIARY or INTELLIGENCE SUMMARY.

Army Form C. 2118.

34th Div. F.A. W.C.

Place	Date	Hour	Summary of Events and Information	Remarks and references to Appendices
ROUEN	12-1-16		Interpreter JULIEN BLANCHARD joined unit. Company, lorry, ambulances, cars, & motor cycles inspected by LIEUT-COL HAYTER, A.D.T. ROUEN. Company trekked to BLANGY at 2-30 p.m. arriving at 5 p.m. and parked for night of 12th-13th.	

Capt. A.S.C.
O.C. 34th Div. Supply Column

WAR DIARY or INTELLIGENCE SUMMARY.

Army Form C. 2118.

34th Divl. T. a. W. u

Place	Date	Hour	Summary of Events and Information	Remarks and references to Appendices
BLANGY	13-1-16		Company resumed trek, leaving BLANGY at 9 am. arrived at ARQUES at 5 P.M. & parked for night of 13th-14th. Reported on road at ABBEVILLE to Camp Commandant	

J. P. [signature] Capt. A.S.C.
O/C 34th Divl. Supply Column

WAR DIARY
or
INTELLIGENCE SUMMARY.

Army Form C. 2118.

34th Divl. F.A.W.U.

Place	Date	Hour	Summary of Events and Information	Remarks and references to Appendices
ARCQUES	14-1-16		Company resumed trek, leaving ARCQUES at 9 a.m., arrived at RENESCURE at 10 a.m. 17 N.C.Os + men, 7 Ambulances Nos A.18324; A.18317; A.18325; A.18326; A.18328; A.18331; A.18328. 1 Motor Cycle No. C.22590 proceeded to WARDRECQUES and were attached to 102nd Field Ambulance, 102nd Brigade for duty. 17 N.C.Os + men, 7 Ambulances Nos A.18321; A.18315; A.18320; A.18313; A.18314; A.18330; A.18327; 1 Motor Cycle No. C.22569 proceeded to FERSINGHEIM and were attached to 103rd Field Ambulance, 103rd Brigade for duty.	

Capt. A.S.C.
O.C. 34th Divl. Supply Column

WAR DIARY
or
INTELLIGENCE SUMMARY.

Army Form C. 2118.

34th Div. A.S.C.

Place	Date	Hour	Summary of Events and Information	Remarks and references to Appendices
RENESCURE	20-1-16		15-1-16 to 19-1-16 Nothing of importance occurred to record. 20-1-16 Interpreter JULIEN BLANCHARD left Unit to join 22 Northumberland Fusiliers. [signature] Capt. A.S.C. O.C. 34th Div. Supply Column	

WAR DIARY or INTELLIGENCE SUMMARY.

Army Form C. 2118.

34th Div. F.A.W.U.

Place	Date	Hour	Summary of Events and Information	Remarks and references to Appendices
RENESCURE	22-1-16		21-1-16. Nothing of importance occurred to record. Officer Commanding, 3 N.C.Os, 4 men, 7 Ambulances, 3 lorries, 1 Car, 1 Motorcycle left RENESCURE at 10 a.m. & proceeded to MORBECQUE at 1-30 p.m. 17 N.C.Os & men, 7 Ambulances - Nos. A.18315; A.18314; A.18332; A.1843; A.1836; A.18329; A.18332. 1 Motorcycle - No. C.27588 were attached to 101st Field Ambulance. 101st Brigade for duty. O.C. 2 N.C.Os & 17 men, 1 Car No. M.18333, 1 Workshop Lorry 21071, 1 Store Lorry 21070, 1 Daimler 30cwt Supply Lorry 21072 form a new A.S.C. Workshop Unit. This Unit is now attached as follows:— 14-1-16. 3 N.C.Os. 4 men, 7 Ambulances, 1 Motorcycle attached 102nd Brigade. 14-1-16. 3 N.C.Os. 4 men, 7 Ambulances, 1 Motorcycle attached 103rd Brigade. 22-1-16. 3 N.C.Os. 4 men, 7 Ambulances, 1 Motorcycle attached 101st Brigade. 22-1-16. O.C., 2 N.C.Os. 17 men, 3 lorries, 1 Car - Sub Ambulance Workshop Unit.	

Capt. A.S.C.
O.C. 34th Div. Supply Column

WAR DIARY or **INTELLIGENCE SUMMARY**.
(Erase heading not required.)

Army Form C. 2118.

34th Div. Train.

Place	Date	Hour	Summary of Events and Information	Remarks and references to Appendices
MORBECQUE	26-1-16		23-1-16 to 25-1-16. Nothing of importance occurred to record. Officer Commanding, 3 N.C.Os & 17 men, Workshop lorry, Store lorry & 30 cwt Daimler Supply lorry proceeded to ESTAIRES. 27-1-16 to 31-1-16 Nothing of importance occurred to record. M.C. O.S. & men, Company were paid.	

J.B. Brackfield Capt. A.S.C.
O/C 34th Div. Supply Column

# WAR DIARY or INTELLIGENCE SUMMARY.

Army Form C. 2118.

Place	Date	Hour	Summary of Events and Information	Remarks and references to Appendices
			Confidential

War Diary

of

3rd Divisional Field Ambulance Workshop Unit

From 1st February to 29th February 1916

(Volume 1) | |

Place	Date	Hour	Summary of Events and Information	Remarks and references to Appendices
ESTAIRES	21-2-16		1-2-16 to 20-2-16 Nothing of importance occurred to record. Officer Commanding evacuated to No.2 London Casualty Clearing Station. M/132633 Private Morris W.H. officer's batman accompanies Officer Commanding to No.2 London Casualty Clearing Station. Unit temporarily placed under supervision of O.C. 8th Divisional Supply Column. Unit under orders to proceed to HOLLEBECK FARM, near STEENWERCK	

J.P. Buckleed Capt. A.S.C.
O.C. 34th Divl. Supply Column

WAR DIARY
or
INTELLIGENCE SUMMARY.
(Erase heading not required.)

Army Form C. 2118.

34th Div. J.a.W.U

Place	Date	Hour	Summary of Events and Information	Remarks and references to Appendices
ESTAIRES.	22-2-16		Orders to proceed to HOLLEBECK FARM cancelled. Unit ordered to proceed to STEENWERCK and be attached to 34th. Divisional Supply Column.	

Capt A.S.C.
O/C 34th. Div. Supply Column.

WAR DIARY
or
INTELLIGENCE SUMMARY
(Erase heading not required.)

Army Form C. 2118.

34th Divl- F.A.W.U.

Place	Date	Hour	Summary of Events and Information	Remarks and references to Appendices
ESTAIRES	24-2-16		23-2-16 Nothing of importance occurred to record. Unit proceeded to STEENWERCK:- O.C. 8th Divisional Supply Column, 3 N.C.O's, 16 men, 1 Workshop Lorry, 1 Store Lorry, 1, 30 cwt Daimler Supply Lorry, & 1 car of 34th Divl. Field Ambulance Workshop Unit. Unit attached to 34th Divisional Supply Column. 25-2-16 to 29-2-16. Nothing of importance occurred to record.	

J.P. Brikett(?) Capt. A.S.C.
O/C 34th Divl-Supply Column

WAR DIARY
or
INTELLIGENCE SUMMARY.
(Erase heading not required.)

Army Form C. 2118.

34 F A W U

Vol 3

Place	Date	Hour	Summary of Events and Information	Remarks and references to Appendices

Confidential

War Diary

of

34th Divisional Field Ambulance Workshop Unit

From 1st March 1916 to 31st March 1916

(Volume 1)

WAR DIARY
INTELLIGENCE SUMMARY.
(Erase heading not required.)

Army Form C. 2118.

34th Divl. F.A.W.U.

Place	Date	Hour	Summary of Events and Information	Remarks and references to Appendices
STEENWERCK	3/16		1-3-16 to 5-3-16 Nothing of importance occurred to report	

P. Mathews 2nd Lt. ASC
O.C. 34th Divl. F.A.W.U.

WAR DIARY or INTELLIGENCE SUMMARY.

Army Form C. 2118.

34th. Divl. T.a.W.u.

Place	Date	Hour	Summary of Events and Information	Remarks and references to Appendices
STEENWERCK	6/3/16		M7/116560 Pte. Perry, P.K., M7/132677 Pte. PATTERSON. P.J., M7/132702 Pte. SANDFORD G. proceeded with Workshop Lorry No ↑ 21471 to ERQUINGHEM	
			1 Car No M ↑ 18333 temporarily transferred to Divisional Headquarters.	

P. Matthew 2nd L. A.S.C.
O/c 34th. Divl. T.a.W.u

WAR DIARY or INTELLIGENCE SUMMARY.

Army Form C. 2118.

34th Div. T-a.w.u

Place	Date	Hour	Summary of Events and Information	Remarks and references to Appendices
STENWERCK	7/3/16		M/116560 Pte PERRY. G.H, M/132677 Pte PATTERSON, M/132702 Pte SANDFORD. G. returned with Workshop Lorry No. T21471 from ERQUINGHEM to STEENWERCK.	

P. Mathews 2nd Lt A.S.C.
o/c 34th Div. T a.w.u

WAR DIARY

INTELLIGENCE SUMMARY.

(Erase heading not required.)

Army Form C. 2118.

34th Div. Dawn

Place	Date	Hour	Summary of Events and Information	Remarks and references to Appendices
STEENWERCK	8/3/16		8/3/16 to 13/3/16. Nothing of importance occurred to report.	
	14/3/16		M7/132387 Pte WEBB A.G. temporarily transferred to Divisional Headquarters.	

P. Mathews 2nd Lt. A.C.C.
to 34th Div. T.A.W.U

WAR DIARY / INTELLIGENCE SUMMARY.

Army Form C. 2118.

34th Divl. F.A.W.u

Place	Date	Hour	Summary of Events and Information	Remarks and references to Appendices
STEENWERCK	17/3/16		15-3-16 to 16-3-16. Nothing of importance occurred to report. 2nd Lt P.H.A. MATTHEWS - O/C and M⁷/132633 Pte MORRIS.W.L rejoined Unit from No 2 London Casualty Clearing Station.	

P. Matthews 2nd Lt. A.S.C.
O/c 34th Divl. F.A.W.u

WAR DIARY or INTELLIGENCE SUMMARY.

Army Form C. 2118.

34th Div. F a W u

Place	Date	Hour	Summary of Events and Information	Remarks and references to Appendices
STEENWERCK	19/3/16		19-3-16. Nothing of importance occurred to report. O/Commanding, 2 N.C.Os & men, 3 lorries Nos. M21470, M21471, M21472 & 1 motor car No. MA18333 trekked from STEENWERCK 28.B.20.a.+b. Sheet 36 and parked at FME DECHERF.	

P. McPherson 2nd A.S.C.
OC. 34th Div. F a W u

WAR DIARY
or
INTELLIGENCE SUMMARY.

Army Form C. 2118.

34th Div. F a w u

Instructions regarding War Diaries and Intelligence Summaries are contained in F. S. Regs., Part II. and the Staff Manual respectively. Title pages will be prepared in manuscript.

(*Erase heading not required.*)

Place	Date	Hour	Summary of Events and Information	Remarks and references to Appendices
STEENWERCK	31/3/16		20-3-16 to 30-3-16 Nothing of importance occurred to report. O/Commanding, 20 N.C.O's + men, 3 lorries nos. ↑21470, ↑21471, ↑21472, and 1 Motor Car No. M↑18333 trekked from FME DECHERF to STEENWERCK + were transferred to the Establishment of the 34th. Div. Supply Column. Authority G.R.O. 1484 dated 30-3-16.	

P. Math, 2nd Lt a.S.C.
9c 34th Div. F a w u